DEPARTMENT OF JUSTICE

Reflections on Antitrust Enforcement in the Obama Administration

BILL BAER
Assistant Attorney General
Antitrust Division
U.S. Department of Justice

Remarks as Prepared for Delivery to the
New York State Bar Association

New York, New York

January 30, 2014

Good evening and thank you, Molly, for your warm introduction. Thanks also to the New York State Bar Association for inviting me to speak tonight. It is a privilege to be here with so many outstanding antitrust practitioners, including tonight's honorees, Professor Eleanor Fox and Jay Himes. Congratulations to you both.

I arrived at the Antitrust Division about a year ago. As I look ahead to the opportunities and challenges facing the division, I think it a good time to review what this talented and hard-working group of public servants—who have braved undeserved pay freezes, budget cuts, and government shutdowns—has accomplished over the past five years of antitrust enforcement during the Obama administration.

I want to make three preliminary observations.

First, for many years—including these last five—antitrust enforcement has been successfully non-partisan. There is important continuity between the efforts of our predecessors, both Republican and Democratic, and the Antitrust Division's current enforcement efforts and policies. Political affiliation means little in this job. Prior Assistant Attorneys General and I share the goal of protecting competition and consumers by making sound and factually supported law-enforcement decisions. Of course, our judgment calls occasionally may differ in some cases and on some issues, but I believe the similarities in goals and methods vastly outweigh those differences.

Second, in returning to public service after a 13-year hiatus, I was reminded of the importance of the Antitrust Division's close partnership with our enforcement colleagues at the Federal Trade Commission (FTC). This should not be a stunning observation, but sometimes the occasional clearance dispute obscures just how much and how well we work together. Whether it is the revised merger guidelines, healthcare and intellectual property guidance, or promoting sound, transparent, and equitable antitrust enforcement internationally, we are partners in significant and lasting respects. I am honored to team with Chairwoman Edith Ramirez and her talented colleagues on these issues. We applaud—and the department was proud to support—the FTC's important victories in the Supreme Court this past term in the *Actavis* and *Phoebe Putney* cases.[1]

---

[1] FTC v. Actavis, Inc., 133 S. Ct. 2223 (2013); FTC v. Phoebe Putney Health Sys., Inc., 133 S. Ct. 1003 (2013).

Third, I claim no personal credit for the division's achievements that I highlight tonight. That credit goes to a quality team of dedicated career professionals and to Assistant Attorney General Christine Varney and the talented lawyers and economists who have honored the division with their service over the last five years. Our current front office team—Renata, Leslie, Aviv, David, Brent, Terrell, Sonia and I—thank them for leaving antitrust enforcement in a strong position. We salute as well the leadership and support of Attorney General Eric Holder—he has been with us every step of the way.

With those preliminary observations in mind, let me focus on the progress antitrust enforcement has made these last five years. President Obama promised during his first campaign that his administration would vigorously enforce the antitrust laws.[2] He pledged to "step up review of merger activity," "take aggressive action to curb the growth of international cartels," and "ensure that the benefits of competition are fully realized by consumers."[3]

I think the record shows the Antitrust Division has followed through on the President's pledge.

Criminal enforcement provides an excellent starting point. We continue to vigorously pursue and prosecute international and domestic cartels. Since January 2009, we have filed 339 criminal cases, a more than 60 percent increase over the prior five years. We secured $4.2 billion in criminal fines in that period. Many people do not appreciate that these dollars do not recycle into our antitrust enforcement budget. Instead they go into the Crime Victim's Fund, which aids Americans harmed by all types of crimes across the nation.[4] The fund provides victims with shelter, crisis intervention, and assistance with medical and counseling expenses, among other services.[5]

---

[2] *See* Barack Obama, Sen., Statement of Senator Barack Obama for the American Antitrust Institute 1 (Sept. 27, 2007), *available at* http://www.antitrustinstitute.org/files/aai-%20Presidential%20campaign%20-%20Obama%209-07_092720071759.pdf.

[3] *Id.*

[4] *See* Fact Sheet, Office for Victims of Crime, U.S. Dep't of Justice, Crime Victims Fund (June 2013), *available at* http://www.ovc.gov/pubs/crimevictimsfundfs/intro.html.

[5] *Id.*

Effective cartel enforcement requires holding accountable both corporations and the senior executives who orchestrate their unlawful conduct. We have charged 109 corporations with criminal antitrust violations since 2009. We have ensured that those corporations have paid appropriate—and stiff—criminal fines, and those 109 corporations together have paid the highest five-year fine total in division history.

The division also charged 311 individuals with antitrust crimes during the past five years. Experience teaches that the threat of prison time is the most effective deterrent against criminal antitrust violations. We seek sentences commensurate with the economic harm caused by the perpetrators. The statistics show that the courts are embracing the effort to hold company executives accountable for their bad behavior. The average prison sentence in our cases has increased from 20 months in the period 2000-09 to 25 months during the years 2010-2013.

Of course, we can never know for certain the full deterrent effect of our enforcement efforts. But we do know that self-reporting under our leniency program remains at high levels and that, increasingly, non-U.S. companies are reporting anticompetitive behavior. They are responding to the fact we are prosecuting off-shore conduct with a U.S. impact. In recent years the number of foreign nationals sentenced to U.S. incarceration has increased threefold. The message should be clear: the division will vigorously and successfully prosecute international cartel behavior that harms U.S. consumers regardless of where that conduct takes place.

As I detailed late last year in joint testimony with the FBI before the Subcommittee on Antitrust, Competition Policy and Consumer Rights of the Senate Judiciary Committee, our partnership with the bureau is key to successful investigation and prosecution of economic crimes.[6] By making increased use of the bureau's expertise and talent, we are better able to uncover unlawful behavior that harms American consumers.

The division has brought criminal cases in a range of industries over the past several years. One of our most significant ongoing investigations involves the auto parts industry. We are prosecuting price fixing and bid rigging involving a number

---

[6] *See Cartel Prosecution: Stopping Price Fixers and Protecting Consumers Before the S. Subcomm. on Antitrust, Competition Policy and Consumer Rights, Comm. on the Judiciary,* 113th Cong. (2013) (statement of William J. Baer, Assistant Att'y Gen., Antitrust Div., U.S. Dep't of Justice), *available at* http://www.justice.gov/atr/public/testimony/301680.pdf.

of parts that were installed in cars sold in the U.S., including wire harnesses, instrument panel clusters, and seatbelts. This chart, which I used in my recent Senate testimony, identifies the component parts caught up in this web of conspiratorial conduct.[7]

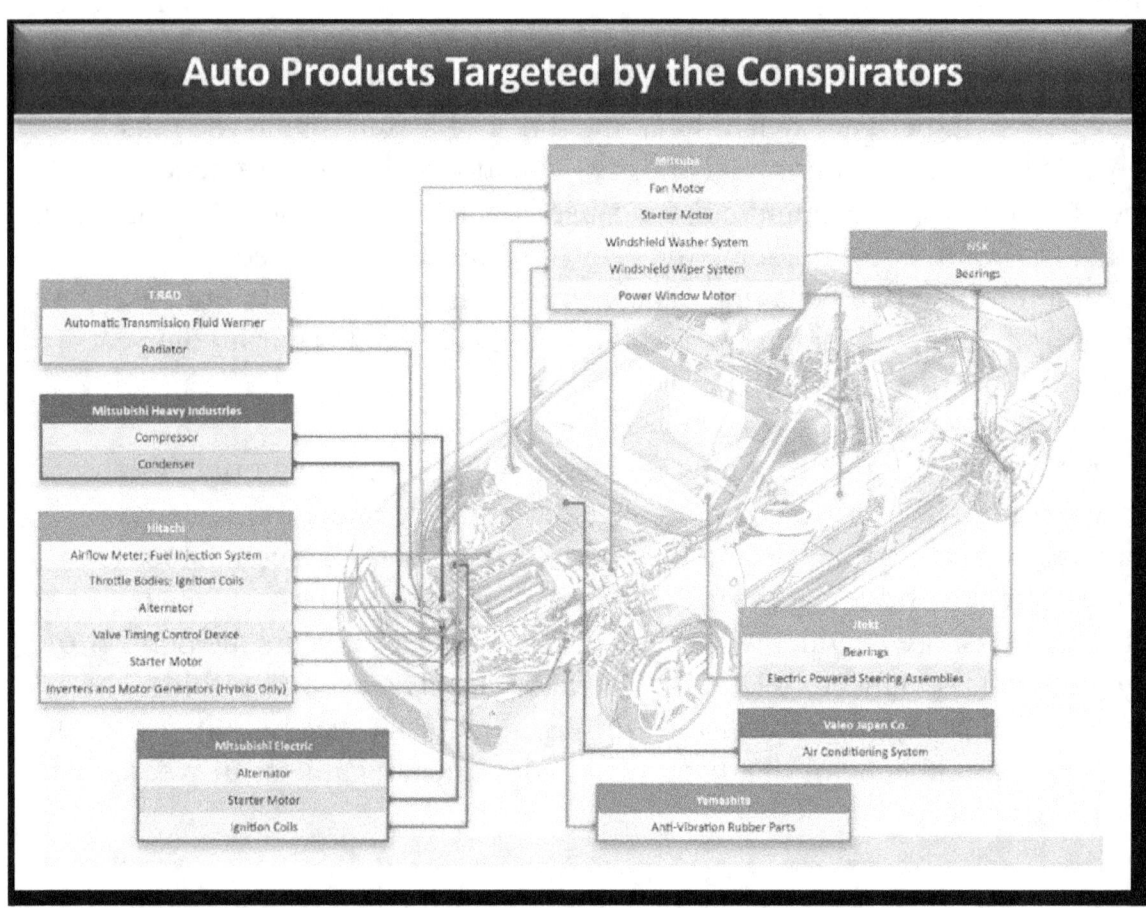

To date, we have charged 24 companies and 26 executives with participating in multiple international conspiracies, and those numbers are sure to grow as the investigation continues.[8] These charges have resulted in $1.8 billion in criminal fines, including the third-largest criminal antitrust fine ever.[9] Of the 26 executives

---

[7] *Id.*

[8] *See* Press Release, U.S. Dep't of Justice, Koito Manufacturing Co. Ltd. Agrees to Plead Guilty to Price Fixing on Automobile Parts Installed in U.S. Cars (Jan. 16, 2014), *available at* http://www.justice.gov/opa/pr/2014/January/14-at-049.html.

[9] *Id.*; Antitrust Div., U.S. Dep't of Justice, Antitrust Division 2013 Criminal Enforcement Update (Spring 2013), *available at* http://www.justice.gov/atr/public/division-update/2013/criminal-program.html [hereinafter Division Spring 2013 Update].

charged so far, 20 have been sentenced to serve time in U.S. prisons or have entered into plea agreements requiring significant sentences.[10]

During the past several years, the division also prosecuted international price-fixing conspiracies involving liquid crystal display panels. These conspiracies hurt U.S. consumers by dramatically inflating prices for computer monitors, notebook computers, and televisions, among other products. In 2012, the division secured convictions of Taiwan-based AU Optronics, its subsidiary, AU Optronics Corp. America, and three former top executives for their participation in such a conspiracy.[11] The trial against AU Optronics was the first time the division proceeded under the alternative fine statute, 18 U.S.C. § 1571, which allows for fines up to two times the gain or loss resulting from the conduct. The division proved beyond a reasonable doubt to the jury that the combined gains to the participants in the conspiracy were $500 million or more and that the defendants' conduct accordingly merited a fine exceeding the Sherman Act's $100 million maximum.[12]

Another recent matter that has resulted in guilty pleas and a trial victory for the division is our investigation into a conspiracy to fix rates for coastal water freight transportation between the continental U.S. and Puerto Rico.[13] This scheme harmed consumers in Puerto Rico who rely on goods imported from the mainland U.S., including food, medicine, and other consumer items. Three companies and six individuals have pleaded guilty or been convicted at trial in the course of this

---

[10] *See* Press Release, U.S. Dep't of Justice, Toyo Tire & Rubber Co. Ltd. Agrees to Plead Guilty to Price Fixing on Automobile Parts Installed in U.S. Cars (Nov. 26, 2013), *available at* http://www.justice.gov/atr/public/press_releases/2013/301891.htm.

[11] *See* Press Release, U.S. Dep't of Justice, AU Optronics Executive Convicted for Role in LCD Price-Fixing Conspiracy (Dec. 18, 2012), *available at* http://www.justice.gov/atr/public/press_releases/2012/290399.htm; Press Release, U.S. Dep't of Justice, Taiwan-Based AU Optronics Corporation, its Houston-Based Subsidiary and Former Top Executives Convicted for Role in LCD Price-Fixing Conspiracy (Mar. 13, 2012), *available at* http://www.justice.gov/atr/public/press_releases/2012/281032.htm.

[12] *See* Press Release, U.S. Dep't of Justice, Taiwan-Based AU Optronics Corporation, its Houston-Based Subsidiary and Former Top Executives Convicted for Role in LCD Price-Fixing Conspiracy (Mar. 13, 2012), *available at* http://www.justice.gov/atr/public/press_releases/2012/281032.htm.

[13] *See, e.g.*, Press Release, U.S. Dep't of Justice, Former Sea Star Line President Sentenced to Serve Five Years in Prison for Role in Price-Fixing Conspiracy Involving Coastal Freight Services between the Continental United States and Puerto Rico (Dec. 6, 2013), *available at* http://www.justice.gov/atr/public/press_releases/2013/302027.htm.

investigation and $46 million in fines have been imposed.[14] The culpable executives have been sentenced to jail terms ranging from seven months to five years.[15] Trial against a seventh individual is scheduled for this May.

Price-fixing and collusion are not limited to tangible goods. As many of you know, recent division prosecutions have shown that financial services markets also are susceptible to unlawful conspiracies that will trigger vigorous antitrust prosecution.

Bid-rigging in municipal bond markets is one example. Working with the FBI and the Internal Revenue Service's Criminal Investigation Division, the Antitrust Division—led by the folks in our New York Office—uncovered and prosecuted conspiracies to defraud municipalities across the nation by manipulating the competitive bidding process for the investment of tax-exempt bond proceeds. These illegal schemes reduce the amount of money that cities and towns can spend on civic projects, such as hospitals and schools, road repair, and affordable housing. Twenty individuals have been charged in this investigation so far and 16 have been convicted or pleaded guilty.[16] One corporation also has pleaded guilty.[17] These prosecutions resulted in $745 million in restitution, penalties, and disgorgement to federal and state agencies.[18]

The division also has cooperated with the FBI and the Criminal Division in prosecuting manipulation of the London Interbank Offered Rate, known as LIBOR. Our coordinated effort exposed schemes to rig benchmark interest rates in order to improve the trading positions of certain financial institutions. This pernicious conduct undermines confidence in the financial markets, which still are recovering from the 2008 financial crisis. To date the department has charged eight individuals and reached resolutions with four banks in this matter. The total

---

[14] *Id.*

[15] *Id.*

[16] *See, e.g.,* Press Release, U.S. Dep't of Justice, Three Former UBS Executives Sentenced to Serve Time in Prison for Frauds Involving Contracts Related to the Investment of Municipal Bond Proceeds (July 24, 2013), *available at* http://www.justice.gov/atr/public/press_releases/2013/299604.htm.

[17] *Id.*

[18] *See* Division Spring 2013 Update, *supra* note 9.

global criminal and regulatory fines, penalties and disgorgement obtained in this investigation are over $3.5 billion.[19]

We remain concerned about fraud and manipulation of financial markets. Just recently, the department publicly confirmed a new joint Antitrust Division and Criminal Division investigation into collusion in foreign exchange markets.

Cartel enforcement is demanding and resource-intensive. And the criminal conduct is not limited to international cartelists. When the Antitrust Division consolidated its field offices three years ago, we committed to continued pursuit of local and regional antitrust violators. We are honoring that pledge. Indeed, with the budget crisis behind us, we are adding prosecutorial staff to our DC office to pursue these crimes.

The real estate market is one place where consumers have been victimized. As part of the Justice Department's commitment to fight financial fraud, the division and the FBI uncovered multiple conspiracies involving bid rigging and fraud at real estate foreclosure auctions in multiple states. These schemes exploited the housing market collapse that followed the 2008 financial crisis. Conspirators bought foreclosed properties at non-competitive prices, victimizing both financial institutions and home owners. So far, the investigation has resulted in charges against 70 individuals and three companies. Sixty-seven individuals have pleaded or agreed to plead guilty to these charges.[20] As we take a number of these cases to trial, you will see the results of the hard investigative work that uncovered this highly problematic conduct. The division also continues to prosecute individuals and entities who have conspired to rig bids at municipal tax lien auctions.[21]

---

[19] *See e.g.,* Press Release, U.S. Dep't of Justice, Three Former Rabobank Traders Charged with Manipulating Yen LIBOR (Jan. 13, 2014), *available at* http://www.justice.gov/atr/public/press_releases/2014/302973.htm.

[20] *See, e.g.,* Press Release, U.S. Dep't of Justice, Three Northern California Real Estate Investors Agree to Plead Guilty to Bid Rigging at Public Foreclosure Auctions (Jan. 2, 2014), *available at* http://www.justice.gov/atr/public/press_releases/2014/302717.htm; Press Release, U.S. Dep't of Justice, Eastern California Real Estate Investor Pleads Guilty to Bid Rigging and Fraud at Public Real Estate Foreclosure Auctions (Dec. 30, 2013), *available at* http://www.justice.gov/atr/public/press_releases/2013/302678.htm.

[21] *See* Press Release, U.S. Dep't of Justice, Six Investors Indicted for their Roles in Bid Rigging Scheme at Municipal Tax Lien Auctions in New Jersey (Nov. 19, 2013), *available at* http://www.justice.gov/atr/public/press_releases/2013/301767.htm.

There is more to come. Our criminal prosecutors in D.C., San Francisco, Chicago and here in New York are working under the guidance of Brent Snyder, our new Deputy Assistant Attorney General for Criminal Enforcement, to pursue a wide range of domestic and international cartelists.

There can be little doubt that the division vigorously prosecutes wrongdoers. But we respect the rights of those under investigation. That is why, after a thorough review of the division's policies regarding corporate plea agreements, I announced last year certain changes to the division's approach to non-prosecution protection for company employees.[22] The new policy provides that in negotiating corporate dispositions, the division will continue to exclude from non-prosecution protection— or "carve out"—employees the division believes to be culpable.[23] But the division no longer carves out employees for reasons unrelated to culpability.[24] And the division no longer includes the names of these likely targets in publicly available plea agreements. Instead, the names are listed in an appendix, which the division seeks to file under seal.[25] So far the division's requests to file under seal the names of individuals carved-out of corporate plea agreements have been granted by the courts in 15 cases. Public disclosure is appropriate if and when we file charges. We appreciate the judiciary's embrace of our effort to respect the rights of the unaccused.

Like cartel enforcement, merger review is central to the division's mission. Unlawful mergers restrain competition, resulting in higher prices, lower quality goods and services, and reduced consumer choice. Over the past five years, the division has shown that it will take all steps necessary to challenge anticompetitive transactions.

In some cases that means filing a lawsuit and proceeding to trial. Two recent trial victories illustrate the division's willingness to litigate and block anticompetitive mergers. Just this month, the division prevailed at trial in its challenge to Bazaarvoice's $168 million consummated acquisition of

---

[22] *See* Press Release, U.S. Dep't of Justice, Statement of Assistant Attorney General Bill Baer on Changes to Antitrust Division's Carve-Out Practice Regarding Corporate Plea Agreements (Apr. 12, 2013), *available at* http://www.justice.gov/atr/public/press_releases/2013/295747.htm.

[23] *Id.*

[24] *Id.*

[25] *Id.*

PowerReviews, its closest rival in the U.S. market for Internet product ratings and reviews platforms.[26] The outcome reinforces a number of key aspects of merger enforcement:

- An anticompetitive transaction that is not reportable under Hart-Scott-Rodino and is already consummated still is subject to Section 7 challenge;
- Where, as here, the evidence of an effort to deny consumers the benefits of competition is strong, the division will act;
- Post-merger evidence of competitive effects that could arguably be subject to manipulation is entitled to little weight; and,
- As Judge Orrick's thoughtful opinion explains, the antitrust laws apply with full force to transactions in the high-technology sector.[27]

We look forward to working with the court in fashioning appropriate remedies to undo the harms caused by Bazaarvoice's misconduct.

In 2011, the division successfully enjoined H&R Block from acquiring TaxAct, its competitor in the market for digital do-it-yourself tax preparation software.[28] The division proved that combining the second- and third-largest competitors would substantially lessen competition in this market, which affects tens of millions of U.S. taxpayers. Indeed, since our trial victory, the market has become more competitive—all three major competitors have launched mobile apps and now couple live tax consultation services with digital do-it-yourself products at no extra charge.[29]

---

[26] United States v. Bazaarvoice, Inc., No. 13-00133, 2014 U.S. Dist. LEXIS 3284 (N.D. Cal. 2014).

[27] *Id.* at 133 ("The fact that social commerce and eCommerce tastes and products are developing and constantly changing does not diminish the applicability of the antitrust laws—they apply in full force in any market. There is no antitrust exemption that allows the market-leading company in a highly concentrated market to buy its closest competitor, even within the evolving social commerce space, when the effect is likely to be anticompetitive.").

[28] United States v. H&R Block, 831 F. Supp. 2d 27 (D.D.C. 2011).

[29] *See, e.g.*, Margaret Collins, *TurboTax Offers Live Tax Advice to Lure Clients from H&R Block*, BLOOMBERG, Feb. 14, 2012, *available at* http://www.bloomberg.com/news/2012-02-14/turbotax-army-of-tax-guides-offers-free-aid-to-lure-clients-from-h-r-block.html; Eileen AJ Connelly, *Live Online Tax Prep Help Sign of Competitive 2012*, MAINSTREET, Dec. 9, 2011, *available at* http://www.mainstreet.com/article/moneyinvesting/taxes/live-online-tax-prep-help-sign-competitive-2012; *Help Topics: Phone Support – Consumer Editions*, TAXACT,

Merger litigation is costly and time consuming. But the last few years demonstrate that we will not hesitate to challenge in court anticompetitive transactions where that is the right course. Of course, the division is always open to meaningful settlement offers from parties that resolve our competitive concerns—both before and after we have sued to block a deal. But the key point is that we will continue to reject settlement terms that do not ensure consumers the benefit of a competitive market.

For example, last year we rejected an inadequate settlement offer from the parties and sued to stop Anheuser-Busch InBev's (ABI) proposed acquisition of total ownership and control of a leading rival and aggressive competitor—Grupo Modelo. Our investigation showed that the transaction would have reduced competition in the U.S. beer market, leading to higher prices. After we sued, the parties quickly agreed to divest to Constellation Brands Modelo's entire U.S. business, ensuring that Modelo would remain an independent horizontal competitor to ABI and MillerCoors.[30] This outcome preserves competition in the U.S. beer market and avoids the price increases and significant consumer harm that would have resulted had the original deal gone through.

More recently, the division sued to block the merger between US Airways and American Airlines. The merger guidelines, and courts applying them, warn about the anticompetitive threat of mergers in increasingly concentrated industries.[31] As proposed, this transaction would have reduced competition in air travel—an industry that is increasingly concentrated and oligopolistic—and raised

---

http://www.taxact.com/tsupport/FAQDisplay.asp?Question=20777&txtSearchValue=phone%20support (last visited Mar. 19, 2012) (describing eligibility for free telephone support).

[30] *See* Press Release, U.S. Dep't of Justice, Justice Department Reaches Settlement with Anheuser-Busch Inbev and Grupo Modelo in Beer Case (Apr. 19, 2013), *available at* http://www.justice.gov/atr/public/press_releases/2013/296018.htm.

[31] U.S. DEP'T OF JUSTICE & FED. TRADE COMM'N, HORIZONTAL MERGER GUIDELINES § 5.3 (2010), *available at* http://www.justice.gov/atr/public/guidelines/hmg-2010.pdf [hereinafter MERGER GUIDELINES]("The higher the post-merger HHI and the increase in the HHI, the greater are the Agencies' potential competitive concerns"); *Bazaarvoice*, 2014 U.S. Dist. LEXIS 3284, at *122 (finding a section 7 violation where "Bazaarvoice's acquisition of PowerReviews significantly increased concentration in the already highly concentrated [ratings and reviews] platform market."); United States v. H&R Block, Inc. 833 F. Supp. 2d 36, 80 (D.D.C. 2011) ("the 'merger would result in the elimination of a particularly aggressive competitor in a highly concentrated market, a factor which is certainly an important consideration when analyzing possible competitive effects,'" *quoting* FTC v. Staples, 970 F. Supp. 1066, 1083 (D.D.C 1997)).

prices for consumers. Once again, during our investigation the parties did not offer meaningful structural relief. That attitude changed on the eve of trial. The settlement we then negotiated requires the parties to surrender key assets at capacity-constrained airports across the country—including 138 slots at Reagan National and LaGuardia Airports and multiple gates in Chicago, Boston, Miami, Dallas and Los Angeles.[32] These divestitures will provide non-legacy competitors the opportunity to expand their national footprint and increase system-wide competition to the benefit of the American consumer.

In other cases, parties abandoned their anticompetitive transactions in the face of a division challenge. In 2011, the division sued to block AT&T's proposed acquisition of T-Mobile.[33] After months of litigation, and in light of factually compelling concerns articulated by both the Antitrust Division and the Federal Communications Commission, the parties abandoned the deal.[34] As I note later, since then competition in the wireless sector has flourished and consumers have benefitted.

Similarly, in 2011, NASDAQ and IntercontinentalExchange abandoned their plan to acquire NYSE Euronext after the division informed the parties it planned to challenge the merger.[35] The division determined that the transaction would have combined the only competitors in several businesses critical to the U.S. equities markets, including stock listing services and stock auction services. And, in 2012, 3M Co. abandoned its plan to acquire Avery Dennison's Office and Consumer Products Group after the division told the parties it would sue to block the deal. The parties were close competitors in the sale of adhesive-backed labels and sticky

---

[32] Press Release, U.S. Dep't of Justice, Justice Department Requires US Airways and American Airlines to Divest Facilities at Seven Key Airports to Enhance System-Wide Competition and Settle Merger Challenge (Nov. 12, 2013), *available at* http://www.justice.gov/atr/public/press_releases/2013/301616.htm.

[33] *See* Second Amended Complaint, United States v. AT&T Inc., No. 1:11-1560 (D.D.C. 2011), *available at* http://www.justice.gov/atr/cases/f275700/275756.pdf.

[34] *See* Press Release, U.S. Dep't of Justice, Justice Department Issues Statements Regarding AT&T Inc.'s Abandonment of its Proposed Acquisition of T-Mobile USA Inc. (Dec. 19, 2011), *available at* http://www.justice.gov/atr/public/press_releases/2011/278406.htm.

[35] See Press Release, U.S. Dep't of Justice, NASDAQ OMX Group Inc. and IntercontinentalExchange Inc. Abandon Their Proposed Acquisition of NYSE Euronext after Justice Department Threatens Lawsuit (May 16, 2011), *available at* http://www.justice.gov/atr/public/press_releases/2011/271214.htm.

notes and 3M would have maneuvered to hold a more than 80 percent share of both the labels and sticky notes markets post-merger.

Other recent significant transactions were remedied by settlements before a contested lawsuit became necessary. In 2011, the division entered into a settlement which resolved the competitive problems presented by the proposed joint venture between Comcast and NBC Universal.[36] This settlement included structural and conduct relief that will protect emerging forms of content distribution. In 2010, the division negotiated a remedy in the Ticketmaster/Live Nation matter that protects competition in ticketing for entertainment events.[37]

There are lessons to be learned. In dealing with problematic mergers in concentrated markets during my years at the FTC and here at the division, I have seen some companies and their advisors assume the antitrust agencies will approve a problematic deal so long as the parties offer up a fig-leaf asset divestiture or an unworkable conduct remedy. Often in horizontal mergers the strategy seems to be to eliminate a big rival while proposing a remedy that allows for a small rival or new entrant with limited resources to nip at the heels of the few remaining big players. Experience, our past antitrust enforcement, and our merger guidance should put companies on notice that this strategy is unlikely to succeed. It did not work for AT&T, which abandoned its effort to buy T-Mobile and reportedly paid a massive break-up fee as a result.[38] It did not work for ABI, which apparently thought it could acquire a leading U.S. rival by offering up some modest concessions, but wound up divesting all Grupo Modelo's assets relating to its participation in the U.S. markets, including a state-of the-art Mexican brewery that will be built-out to supply anticipated growth in U.S. demand.

---

[36] *See* Press Release, U.S. Dep't of Justice, Justice Department Allows Comcast-NBCU Joint Venture to Proceed with Conditions (Jan. 18, 2011), *available at* http://www.justice.gov/atr/public/press_releases/2011/266149.pdf. The court approved the final judgment in September 2011. *See* Final Judgment, United States v. Comcast Corp., No. 11-00106 (D.D.C. 2011), *available at* http://www.justice.gov/atr/cases/f274700/274713.pdf.

[37] See Press Release, U.S. Dep't of Justice, Justice Department Requires Ticketmaster Entertainment Inc. to Make Significant Changes to its Merger with Live Nation Inc. (Jan. 25, 2010), *available at* http://www.justice.gov/atr/public/press_releases/2010/254540.pdf. The court approved the Final Judgment in July 2010. *See* United States v.Ticketmaster Entm't, Inc., No. 10-00139 (D.D.C. July 30, 2010), *available at* http://www.justice.gov/atr/cases/f260900/260909.pdf.

[38] Vipal Monga, *AT&T is Paying the Biggest Breakup Fee Ever*, WALL ST. J., DEAL JOURNAL (Dec. 19, 2011, 6:14 PM), *available at* http://blogs.wsj.com/deals/2011/12/19/att-is-paying-the-biggest-breakup-fee-ever/.

As these actions demonstrate, a key lesson from merger enforcement in the Obama administration is that the division will go to court to challenge problematic transactions to get solutions that resolve anticompetitive concerns. We are always open to good faith remedial proposals from parties. But we will not waste our time with plainly inadequate settlement offers. And, merging parties inevitably delay resolution of their matters by not seriously addressing our competitive concerns when proposing settlement terms.

The business community, consumers, and antitrust enforcers all are better off if anticompetitive mergers die on the drawing board. Our Horizontal Merger Guidelines advance that goal.[39] The FTC and the division issued revised guidelines in 2010 following an open and transparent process, which included public workshops and the release of a guidelines draft for public comment. The result is updated guidance that more accurately reflects current merger review practice at the division and the FTC.

Guidance on remedies is important as well. In 2011, the division released an updated Policy Guide to Merger Remedies, which provides insight into current thinking at the division about how to remedy anticompetitive transactions.[40] The policy guide foreshadowed how the division would analyze the divestitures in the US Airways/American Airlines matter. The guide states that the division will not approve a potential divestiture buyer in an oligopolistic market where that course of action increases the likelihood of post-merger coordination.[41] It should come as no surprise then that the divested slots and gates would go to carriers most likely to enhance rather than inhibit competition.

We understand that merger review can be expensive and time-consuming and that most transactions the division reviews are not anticompetitive. We are committed to reducing the burden on merging parties. As part of that effort, the division has expanded its acceptance of cutting-edge document production techniques, like predictive coding, that have the potential to save parties time and money while providing the division with the documents it needs to fully evaluate transactions.

---

[39] U.S. DEP'T OF JUSTICE & FED. TRADE COMM'N, HORIZONTAL MERGER GUIDELINES § 5.3 (2010), *available at* http://www.justice.gov/atr/public/guidelines/hmg-2010.pdf.

[40] U.S. DEP'T OF JUSTICE, ANTITRUST DIVISION POLICY GUIDE TO MERGER REMEDIES (2011), *available at* http://www.justice.gov/atr/public/guidelines/272350.pdf.

[41] *Id.* at 28.

Let me spend a few minutes discussing the real-world significance of effective antitrust enforcement. The audience here tonight consists of experienced and sophisticated antitrust practitioners. Even for this group, antitrust law often can seem abstract and theoretical, due at least in part to the jargon we use and the difficulty we sometimes encounter in articulating how effective enforcement and competitive markets provide real benefits for American consumers.

Some years ago—in an effort to demystify antitrust enforcement—I gave a talk about "The Dollars and Sense of Antitrust Enforcement."[42] Viewing division enforcement over the past few years through that prism is worthwhile. It enables us to look at the tangible ways in which consumers benefit from competitive markets and how anticompetitive mergers and bad conduct threaten those benefits.

Since 2008, the nation has battled a financial crisis and then the resulting deep recession. Many Americans have struggled to make ends meet. Antitrust enforcement has served during this crisis to protect and promote competition in markets that affect the bottom lines of American families. Our actions enforcing the antitrust laws in the e-books, wireless and health care markets are illustrative.

Consider the serious and documented economic harm caused by the e-books conspiracy recently orchestrated by Apple Inc. and certain book publishers. On July 10, 2013, Judge Cote issued a 160 page opinion finding that Apple had violated Section 1 of the Sherman Act by conspiring with publishers to raise e-books prices and to end e-books retailers' freedom to compete on price.[43] Judge Cote found that the conspiracy was effective: the publishers' e-books prices increased across the board once the illegal agreements were in place.[44] Overnight, the price of the defendants' bestselling e-books rose from $9.99 to $12.99 or $14.99.[45] As Judge Cote explained, "from the consumer's perspective . . . the arrival of the iBookstore brought less price competition and higher prices."[46]

---

[42] William J. Baer, Dir., Bureau of Competition, Fed. Trade Comm'n, The Dollars and Sense of Antitrust Enforcement, Remarks before the Antitrust Section of the New York State Bar Association (Jan. 25, 1996), *available at* http://www.ftc.gov/public-statements/1996/01/dollar-and-sense-antitrust-enforcement.

[43] United States v. Apple Inc., 2013 U.S. Dist. LEXIS 96424 (S.D.N.Y. July 10, 2013).

[44] *Id.* at *109-115.

[45] *Id.* at *94-100, 113, 119-120.

[46] *Id.* at *183.

The evidence of consumers benefiting from post-injunction price competition is equally compelling. Current pricing data shows that since injunctions against Apple and its book publisher co-conspirators were entered, the average price of the top 25 best-selling e-books dropped from around $11 to around $6.[47] Further, our state attorneys general partners secured settlements with the publishers that will return more than $160 million to e-books consumers through seamless credits to their accounts.[48] This refund process is already in motion.[49]

The final judgment[50] in the e-books case put a stop to Apple's anticompetitive conduct. Equally important, it established an external compliance monitor to review and evaluate Apple's antitrust compliance policies and procedures, as well as the antitrust training the final judgment requires.[51] External monitors are an important part of civil law enforcement, whether in the antitrust, civil rights or environmental context. And a monitor in this case is especially important—given the record evidence of Apple's unapologetically anticompetitive conduct, the extent of the consumer injury, the involvement in the conspiracy by high-level executives and lawyers, the findings that their sworn testimony lacked credibility,[52] and the absence of a culture of antitrust training and compliance. As Judge Cote has noted, Apple abused the competitive process and injured U.S. consumers.[53] The public is entitled to remedies that will ensure that Apple changes

---

[47] *See, e.g.*, Deanna Utroske, *New All-Time Low Average Price for Best-Selling Ebooks,* DBW DAILY (Sept. 11, 2013), *available at* http://www.digitalbookworld.com/2013/new-all-time-low-average-price-for-best-selling-ebooks/.

[48] *See* Bill Baer, Assistant Att'y Gen., Antitrust Div., U.S. Department of Justice, Remedies Matter: The Importance of Achieving Effective Antitrust Outcomes, Remarks as Prepared for the Georgetown Law 7th Annual Global Antitrust Enforcement Symposium 10 (Sept. 25, 2013), *available at* http://www.justice.gov/atr/public/speeches/300930.pdf.

[49] *See, e.g.*, Customer FAQ for Attorneys General E-book Settlements, AMAZON.COM, INC., http://www.amazon.com/gp/help/customer/display.html/?nodeId=201046060 (last accessed Jan. 26, 2014).

[50] Final Judgment, United States v. Apple Inc., No. 12-2826 (S.D.N.Y. Sept. 5, 2013), *available at* http://www.justice.gov/atr/cases/f300500/300510.pdf.

[51] *Id.* at 19-25.

[52] *See,* Apple Inc., 2013 U.S. Dist. LEXIS 96424, *passim.*

[53] *See, id.* at *114, 141-42, 151-53.

its ways and does not again engage in anticompetitive conduct in the e-book business or any other markets in which it competes.

Evidence from the wireless market also shows the tangible consumer benefits of antitrust enforcement. Since AT&T terminated its effort to eliminate T-Mobile as a rival, T-Mobile has spearheaded increased competition in wireless services. Shortly after the merger was abandoned, T-Mobile announced a $4 billion investment in modernizing its network and deploying 4G LTE service.[54] It then made a series of moves to offer cheaper and better customer contracts, including offering plans without annual contracts and selling Apple's iPhone 5 on better terms than the competition.[55] Just this month, T-Mobile announced a deal with Verizon Wireless to acquire additional spectrum.[56] And T-Mobile recently offered to pay the early termination fees of its competitors' customers, if they switch to T-Mobile.[57]

These moves are paying off. T-Mobile announced gaining 648,000 wireless subscribers in the third quarter of 2013—its second straight quarter of subscriber growth—besting both AT&T and Sprint.[58]

Pushed by T-Mobile, the competition has responded. Sprint began offering unlimited plans with aggressive prices and innovative service arrangements.[59]

---

[54] *See* Greg Bensinger, *T-Mobile to Pump $4 Billion into Network, 4G Buildout*, WALL ST. J., Feb. 24, 2012, *available at* http://online.wsj.com/article/SB10001424052970203918304577241042653586170.html.

[55] *See, e.g.*, Summar Ghias, *T-Mobile Offers Cheap Service Plans for the iPhone 5*, DEALNEWS (Sept. 7, 2013), *available at* http://dealnews.com/features/T-Mobile-Drops-Contracts-Offers-Cheap-Service-Plans-and-70-Off-the-iPhone-5/687731.html; Erica Ogg & Kevin Fitchard, *T-Mobile Tweaks Pricing Again: New 'Zero Down' Plan is Quite the Deal When Combined with Jump*, GIGAOM (July 26 2013), *available at* http://gigaom.com/2013/07/26/t-mobile-tweaks-pricing-again-iphone-5-with-no-down-payment-27-per-month/.

[56] *See* Ryan Knuston & Ben Fox Rubin, *T-Mobile to Buy Airwave Rights from Verizon Wireless*, WALL ST. J., Jan. 6, 2014, *available at* http://online.wsj.com/news/articles/SB10001424052702303433304579304123993681410.

[57] Edward C. Baig, *CES 2014: T-Mobile to Cover Your Early Termination Fee*, USA TODAY, Jan. 10, 2014, *available at* http://www.usatoday.com/story/tech/columnist/baig/2014/01/08/ces-tmobile-early-termination-fee/4379291/.

[58] *See* Thomas Gryta, *T-Mobile Gains More Valuable Subscribers*, WALL ST. J., Nov. 5, 2013, *available at* http://online.wsj.com/news/articles/SB10001424052702303936904579179480677625124.

16

AT&T recently offered T-Mobile customers a $200 credit, plus money for smartphone trade-ins, to switch.[60] And, after T-Mobile announced a plan which allows subscribers to trade in their handsets for an upgraded model twice a year, AT&T, Verizon and Sprint all announced plans that allow customers to upgrade more often.[61] Competition today is driving enormous benefits in the direction of the American consumer.

The division also continues to focus on contractual provisions that artificially increase healthcare costs. With that in mind, in 2010, the division and the Michigan Attorney General's office challenged Blue Cross Blue Shield of Michigan's contracts with health care providers that included most-favored-nation clauses (MFNs).[62] These MFNs caused hospitals to raise their prices to competing health insurers and reduced competition in health insurance. As a result, Michigan consumers paid more for their healthcare. In 2013, after almost two years of litigation, the state of Michigan passed a law prohibiting health insurers from including MFNs in their contracts with health care providers.[63] This law squarely addressed the harm we alleged in our complaint, so we moved to dismiss our case.[64] The message is getting out. Since we brought suit, a number of states have restricted the use of MFNs in insurer contracts with health-care providers. And health insurers in other states have chosen to stop using MFNs in their provider contracts.

---

[59] *See, e.g.*, Joe Arico, *Sprint to Offer Unlimited Plans with iPhone to Gain Advantage*, MOBILEDIA, *available at* http://www.mobiledia.com/news/111101.html.

[60] Press Release, AT&T Inc., AT&T Offers T-Mobile Customers up to $450 per Line to Switch (Jan. 3, 2014), *available at* http://www.att.com/gen/press-room?pid=25181&cdvn=news&newsarticleid=37365.

[61] *See, e.g.*, Roger Cheng, *T-Mobile vs. Sprint: Who Offers a Better Early Upgrade?*, CNET (Sept. 26, 2013), *available at* http://news.cnet.com/8301-1035_3-57604651-94/t-mobile-vs-sprint-who-offers-a-better-early-upgrade/; Marguerite Reardon, *Which Device Early Upgrade Option Offers the Best Value?*, CNET (July 19, 2013), *available at* http://news.cnet.com/8301-1035_3-57594470-94/which-device-early-upgrade-option-offers-the-best-value/.

[62] *See* Complaint, United States v. Blue Cross Blue Shield of Mich., No. 10-15155 (E.D. Mich. 2013), *available at* http://www.justice.gov/atr/cases/f263200/263235.pdf.

[63] 2013 Mich. Pub. Act 5, 97th Cong. (Mich. 2013), *available at* http://legislature.mi.gov/documents/2013-2014/publicact/pdf/2013-PA-0005.pdf.

[64] *See* Press Release, U.S. Dep't of Justice, Justice Department Files Motion to Dismiss Antitrust Lawsuit Against Blue Cross Blue Shield of Michigan after Michigan Passes Law to Prohibit Health Insurers from Using Most Favored Nation Clauses in Provider Contracts (Mar. 25, 2013), *available at* http://www.justice.gov/atr/public/press_releases/2013/295114.htm.

Enforcement actions by the division and the FTC understandably command a lot of public attention. But it is important not to overlook our pro-competition advocacy and our focus on policy issues that we believe have a tangible impact on American consumers. Intellectual property issues involving standards-essential patents and the availability of injunctive relief illustrate the point.

In January 2013, the division teamed with the U.S. Patent and Trademark Office (PTO) to issue a Policy Statement on Remedies for Standards-Essential Patents Subject to Voluntary F/RAND Commitments.[65] That policy statement concluded that in many situations it may not be in the public interest for the U.S. International Trade Commission (ITC) to issue an exclusion order "where the infringer is acting within the scope of the patent holder's F/RAND commitment and is able, and has not refused, to license on F/RAND terms."[66]

A few months later the administration applied the policy to a specific ITC decision. Relying on the analytical framework laid out in the joint Department of Justice/PTO policy statement, the U.S. Trade Representative disapproved an ITC exclusion order that would have halted U.S. sales of certain older-generation Apple products, ensuring that U.S. consumers will continue to have access to more affordable technology.[67] That the division worked so hard to ensure fair treatment for Apple, which itself has been found unwilling to abide by antitrust norms, demonstrates our commitment to even-handed, merits-based antitrust enforcement.

The final topic I want to touch on tonight is international engagement. U.S. antitrust enforcers appreciate that our enforcement actions and policy announcements are watched closely in jurisdictions around the world. The division continues to engage internationally and to promote policy convergence around sound antitrust principles, transparency, procedural fairness and enforcement cooperation. One of tonight's honorees, Professor Eleanor Fox, has made this her life's work. I know she delights in and deserves credit for the progress we have made, both in bi-lateral and multi-lateral forums. Fourteen years ago the Justice Department and the FTC helped found the International

---

[65] U.S. DEP'T OF JUSTICE & U.S. PATENT & TRADEMARK OFFICE, POLICY STATEMENT ON REMEDIES FOR STANDARDS-ESSENTIAL PATENTS SUBJECT TO VOLUNTARY F/RAND COMMITMENTS (2013), *available at* http://www.justice.gov/atr/public/guidelines/290994.pdf.

[66] *Id.* at 9.

[67] Letter from Michael B.G. Froman, Ambassador, U.S. Trade Rep., to Irving A. Williamson, Chairman, U.S. Int'l Trade Comm'n, at 2 (Aug. 3, 2013), *available at* http://www.ustr.gov/sites/default/files/08032013%20Letter_1.PDF.

Competition Network (ICN). At last count the ICN had nearly 130 members from 111 jurisdictions.[68] The division, along with the FTC, is also an active participant in the Organisation for Economic Co-operation and Development (OECD), and I am privileged to chair OECD Working Party 3 on cooperation and enforcement.

Much of the division's international engagement takes place in the context of its bi-lateral relationships. During the past few years, we have worked hard to cultivate and deepen those relationships. We meet regularly with our good friends and partners in the European Commission (EC) and we have enhanced that relationship over the past years. In 2011, the division, the FTC, and the EC celebrated the 20th anniversary of the U.S.-EU bi-lateral antitrust agreement and issued an updated set of best practices to coordinate their merger reviews.[69]

During the Obama administration U.S. enforcers have broken new ground in relations with China and India. In the past few years, the division and the FTC have entered into Memoranda of Understanding (MOU) with the Chinese and Indian enforcement agencies.[70] These MOUs have led to annual bi-lateral meetings between the U.S. antitrust enforcement agencies and agencies from these nations. Indeed, earlier this month, I attended with Chairwoman Ramirez a bi-lateral meeting with the Chinese authorities in Beijing. We see candid engagement with the Chinese and Indian agencies as important, and we look forward to increased cooperation in the coming years.

---

[68] Maria Coppola, Counsel for Int'l Antitrust, Fed. Trade Comm'n, *International Competition Network, in* GLOBAL COMPETITION REVIEW, THE ANTITRUST REVIEW OF THE AMERICAS 2014, *available at* http://globalcompetitionreview.com/reviews/54/sections/181/chapters/2135/international-competition-network/.

[69] Antitrust Div., U.S. Dep't of Justice, US-EU Merger Working Group, Best Practices on Cooperation in Merger Investigations (2011), *available at* http://www.justice.gov/atr/public/international/docs/276276.pdf; *see also*, Press Release, U.S. Dep't of Justice, United States and European Union Antitrust Agencies Issue Revised Best Practices for Coordinating Merger Reviews (Oct. 14, 2011), *available at* http://www.justice.gov/atr/public/press_releases/2011/276308.htm.

[70] Memorandum of Understanding on Antitrust and Antimonopoly Cooperation between the United States Department of Justice and Federal Trade Commission, on the One Hand, and The People's Republic of China National Development and Reform Commission, Ministry of Commerce, and State Administration for Industry and Commerce, on the Other Hand (July 27, 2011), *available at* http://www.justice.gov/atr/public/international/docs/273310.pdf; Memorandum of Understanding on Antitrust Cooperation between the United States Department of Justice and the United States Federal Trade Commission, and the Ministry of Corporate Affairs (Government of India) and the Competition Commission of India (Sept. 27, 2012), *available at* http://www.justice.gov/atr/public/international/docs/287457a.pdf.

Cooperation also plays an important role in our international criminal cartel investigations. Working with competition enforcers in non-U.S. jurisdictions, we share information where we are able; and we can plan coordinated raids around the world, reducing the opportunity for key evidence to go missing or be destroyed. For example, the Japanese Fair Trade Commission (JFTC) recently uncovered a conspiracy to fix the prices of bearings sold to car makers in the United States and elsewhere. After the JFTC executed search warrants against the bearings conspirators, a number of the companies involved reported their role in cartel activity affecting the U.S. and offered full cooperation with our investigation. Late last year, the Attorney General announced the first results of these joint efforts as certain bearings conspirators agreed to plead guilty and to pay hefty criminal fines.[71]

Let me conclude with a couple of quick points. The people in this room know better than anyone that antitrust analysis can be a complex undertaking. We need to continue to work on sharpening our analysis and to getting to the right answers on the complex policy and enforcement issues we confront every day. It is not always an easy process, but I believe it is critical to effective antitrust enforcement.

We are proud of what the division has accomplished so far during the Obama administration, but there is much work to be done. We look forward to the challenges the next few years will bring. We aim to build on the energy, vigor and success in protecting competition that have marked antitrust enforcement these past five years.

Thank you.

---

[71] Press Release, U.S. Dep't of Justice, Nine Automobile Parts Manufacturers and Two Executives Agree to Plead Guilty to Fixing Prices on Automobile Parts Sold to U.S. Car Manufacturers and Installed in U.S. Cars (Sept. 26, 2013), *available at* http://www.justice.gov/atr/public/press_releases/2013/300969.htm.